How Can You Unlock the Hero Within

The Entrepreneur's Guide to Success in 2025

CONSULTORIA IA

How Can You Unlock the Hero Within

The Entrepreneur's Guide to Success in 2025

CONSULTORIA IA

Consultoria IA

How Can You Unlock the Hero Within?

The Entrepreneur's Guide to Success in 2025

Copyright © 2024 by Consultoria IA

All rights reserved. No part of this publication may be reproduced, stored or transmitted in any form or by any means, electronic, mechanical, photocopying, recording, scanning, or otherwise without written permission from the publisher. It is illegal to copy this book, post it to a website, or distribute it by any other means without permission.

First edition

This book was professionally typeset on Reedsy

Find out more at reedsy.com

Contents

[How Can You Unlock the Hero Within? The Entrepreneur's Guide to Success in 2025](#)

[Review](#)

[Target Audience](#)

[What this books solve](#)

[Preface](#)

[Chapter 1: The Hero's Mindset – Building Resilience for Uncertainty](#)

[Chapter 2: Navigating the Future – Embracing Technology and Innovation](#)

[Chapter 3: Crafting Your Vision – Turning Dreams into Actionable Goals](#)

[Chapter 4: The Power of Connection – Building Networks That Propel Success](#)

[Chapter 5: Thriving Through Failure – Transforming Setbacks into Opportunities](#)

[Appendices](#)

How Can You Unlock the Hero Within? The Entrepreneur's Guide to Success in 2025

Review

In this inspiring and forward-thinking eBook, the author takes readers on a transformative journey to uncover the "hero" within themselves. Targeted at entrepreneurs striving to succeed in an ever-evolving world, this guide is packed with actionable insights, cutting-edge strategies, and motivational anecdotes.

With a focus on the challenges and opportunities of 2025, the book delves into topics such as personal resilience, leveraging emerging technologies, and cultivating a growth mindset. The author combines practical advice with a storytelling approach, making complex ideas accessible and engaging.

Whether you're a seasoned business owner or just starting out, this eBook serves as both a roadmap and a source of inspiration for achieving success and fulfillment. A must-read for those ready to embrace their inner hero and thrive in the entrepreneurial landscape of tomorrow!

Target Audience

The target audience for *How Can You Unlock the Hero Within? The Entrepreneur's Guide to Success in 2025* includes:

Aspiring Entrepreneurs: Individuals considering starting their own business and seeking guidance on building resilience, leveraging technology, and adopting a success-driven mindset.

Seasoned Entrepreneurs: Established business owners looking for fresh perspectives and strategies to adapt and thrive in a rapidly changing environment.

Professionals Transitioning to Entrepreneurship: Corporate professionals or freelancers exploring entrepreneurial opportunities and needing a motivational and practical roadmap.

Innovation Enthusiasts: Those interested in the future of business, emerging trends, and tools to stay ahead in the competitive marketplace of 2025.

Self-Development Seekers: Individuals focused on personal growth and unlocking their potential, both in life and business, to achieve a more fulfilling career and lifestyle.

What this books solve

How Can You Unlock the Hero Within? The Entrepreneur's Guide to Success in 2025 addresses several key problems faced by entrepreneurs and aspiring business leaders, including:

Lack of Clarity and Direction: Provides a structured framework for identifying personal and business goals, helping readers align their vision with actionable steps.

Overcoming Self-Doubt: Offers strategies to build confidence, embrace challenges, and unlock the "heroic" mindset needed to tackle uncertainty.

Adapting to Rapid Change: Explains how to stay agile and leverage emerging technologies, trends, and business models in a dynamic marketplace.

Burnout and Stress Management: Introduces techniques for balancing personal well-being with professional demands to maintain long-term resilience.

Navigating Competitive Landscapes: Shares insights on standing out in a saturated market, fostering innovation, and creating unique value propositions.

Skill Gaps in Modern Entrepreneurship: Covers essential skills like digital transformation, leadership, and building collaborative networks that are critical for success in 2025.

Fear of Failure: Inspires readers with real-life stories and actionable advice to embrace failures as stepping stones to success.

By addressing these challenges, the book equips readers with the mindset, tools, and strategies to achieve entrepreneurial success in a fast-evolving world.

Preface

As we approach 2025, the world of entrepreneurship stands at the edge of unprecedented transformation. Advances in technology, shifting market dynamics, and evolving customer expectations have created a landscape of both incredible opportunities and formidable challenges. In this rapidly changing environment, success requires more than just business acumen; it demands resilience, creativity, and an unwavering belief in your ability to adapt and thrive.

This book is an invitation to embark on a journey of self-discovery and empowerment. It is not just a guide to navigating the entrepreneurial world—it is a call to awaken the hero within you. Whether you are launching your first venture, scaling an established business, or simply dreaming of making your mark, the tools and insights shared here will equip you to rise above obstacles and turn your vision into reality.

Drawing from personal experiences, real-world examples, and the latest industry trends, this book is designed to inspire action. It will show you how to embrace change, harness innovation, and cultivate the mindset of a leader prepared to succeed in the evolving landscape of 2025 and beyond.

The journey of an entrepreneur is rarely easy, but it is always transformative. Together, let us unlock the hero within you and write the story of your success.

Welcome to your adventure. Let's begin.

Chapter 1: The Hero's Mindset – Building Resilience for Uncertainty

Introduction: Embracing the Hero Within

Every entrepreneur's journey is marked by challenges, unpredictability, and change. In 2025, where technological disruption, economic volatility, and rapid market shifts are the norm, resilience isn't just an advantage—it's a necessity. Developing what we call "The Hero's Mindset" means cultivating the mental fortitude and adaptability to not only face uncertainty but to thrive in it. Let's dive into how you can harness this mindset to unlock your entrepreneurial potential.

The Foundation of Resilience: Why It Matters

Resilience is the ability to recover quickly from setbacks and adapt to change. Think of it as the mental muscle that allows you to weather the storm and come out stronger. Studies from the American Psychological Association show that resilient individuals are more likely to succeed in high-pressure environments. Entrepreneurs face an average of 1.5 significant crises per year—from financial challenges to market disruptions. The ability to bounce back is not optional; it's fundamental.

Key Components of Resilience:
1. Emotional Regulation: Staying calm and focused under pressure.
2. Cognitive Flexibility: Adapting your thinking to new realities.
3. Growth Mindset: Viewing challenges as opportunities to learn and grow.
4. Social Support: Building a network that uplifts and guides you.

Data Insight:

A 2024 survey by McKinsey found that 78% of successful entrepreneurs attributed their ability to pivot during uncertainty to mental resilience.

Practical Strategies for Building Resilience

Building resilience isn't about innate talent; it's about consistent practices. Here are actionable steps you can take to develop your Hero's Mindset:

1. Reframe Failure as Feedback

When things don't go as planned, it's easy to spiral into negativity. Instead, view failure as data. Each setback provides insights into what works and what doesn't. Entrepreneurs like Sara Blakely, founder of Spanx, credit their success to embracing failure. Her philosophy: "Fail big, fail forward."

Quick Tip:

After every setback, ask yourself:
- What went wrong?
- What can I learn?
- How will I improve next time?

Write your answers down. This reflective practice shifts your focus from despair to action.

2. Practice Mental Flexibility with "What If" Scenarios

Uncertainty often triggers fear because we feel unprepared. Combat this by mentally rehearsing different outcomes. Ask yourself:
- "What if my biggest client leaves?"
- "What if the market shifts overnight?"

By brainstorming solutions in advance, you'll feel more equipped to handle surprises when they arise.

Case Study:

When Netflix transitioned from DVD rentals to streaming, they didn't wait for the market to force their hand. They anticipated the change and pivoted proactively, staying ahead of the curve.

3. Build Your "Hero's Toolkit"

Resilience requires tools. Consider these essentials for your entrepreneurial arsenal:

A. Meditation for Mental Clarity:

Meditation reduces stress and improves decision-making. Apps like Headspace or Calm make it easy to start. Research shows that just 10 minutes a day can lower cortisol levels by 20%.

B. Physical Activity for Endurance:

Exercise isn't just about staying fit. It's a proven way to boost mood and energy. A study in Harvard Business Review found that CEOs who exercised regularly were 25% more effective at managing stress.

C. Learning for Adaptability:

Stay curious and open to new ideas. Sign up for courses, read books, or listen to podcasts. Remember, knowledge is power—especially in uncertain times.

Stories of Resilient Entrepreneurs

Stories have the power to inspire and guide. Here are examples of entrepreneurs who exemplified resilience:

1. Elon Musk: Master of Reframing

In 2008, Tesla was on the brink of bankruptcy. Musk faced ridicule, lawsuits, and financial ruin. Yet, instead of giving up, he doubled down. By reframing problems as solvable puzzles, he secured funding, inspired his team, and revolutionized the automotive industry.

2. Oprah Winfrey: The Power of Authenticity

Oprah's early career was fraught with failures—including being fired from her first TV job. Instead of retreating, she used these experiences to shape her unique style, eventually becoming one of the most influential media moguls of our time.

3. Airbnb Founders: The Value of Persistence

When Airbnb launched, they struggled to get traction. Rather than giving up, the founders hustled—selling novelty cereal boxes to fund their startup. Their ability to endure tough times laid the groundwork for a $100 billion company.

Turning Adversity into Opportunity

One hallmark of a resilient entrepreneur is the ability to see opportunity in adversity. This requires a shift in perspective:

1. Look for Hidden Trends

In moments of chaos, patterns often emerge. During the COVID-19 pandemic, industries like e-commerce, remote work, and telehealth boomed. Entrepreneurs who spotted these trends early positioned themselves for massive growth.

Exercise:

Set aside 15 minutes each week to review industry news. Ask yourself:
- What new problems are emerging?
- How can I position my business as the solution?

2. Build a "Plan Z"

Having a contingency plan doesn't mean you expect to fail. It means you're prepared for the unexpected. This reduces anxiety and boosts confidence.

Example:

Reid Hoffman, co-founder of LinkedIn, always emphasizes the importance of a "Plan Z." For him, this meant returning to a stable job if his entrepreneurial ventures failed. Knowing he had a fallback gave him the courage to take risks.

The Role of Community in Resilience

Entrepreneurship can be lonely, but it doesn't have to be. Surrounding yourself with a supportive community is crucial for maintaining resilience.

1. Find Your Tribe

Join networks of like-minded individuals. Whether it's a local business group or an online forum, connecting with others who understand your challenges can provide encouragement and fresh perspectives.

Recommendation:
- Check out platforms like:
  - YEC (Young Entrepreneur Council): Exclusive community of successful entrepreneurs.
  - Indie Hackers: Forum for sharing progress and lessons.

2. Lean on Mentors

Mentorship accelerates growth. A good mentor can provide guidance, share their experiences, and help you navigate uncertainty.

How to Find a Mentor:
- Attend industry events.
- Reach out on LinkedIn with a thoughtful message.
- Offer value first (e.g., share insights or assistance).

Resilience in Action: A Visualization Exercise

A practical exercise. Visualization is a powerful tool to reinforce resilience:

1. Close your eyes and imagine your biggest challenge.
2. Visualize yourself tackling it with confidence. What steps do you take? How do you feel?
3. Now, picture the outcome. See yourself celebrating success.

Repeat this exercise whenever self-doubt creeps in. Over time, you'll train your brain to associate challenges with empowerment instead of fear.

Resilience is not a destination; it's a journey. By adopting the Hero's Mindset, you equip yourself with the tools, habits, and perspective needed to navigate the uncertainties of entrepreneurship in 2025. Remember, every great hero faces trials. What sets them apart is their ability to rise, adapt, and conquer.

The next time you face uncertainty, ask yourself: What would my heroic self do? Then, take action. The world needs your courage, vision, and tenacity.

The Top 3 Challenges for Entrepreneurs: Strategies to Overcome Obstacles

Entrepreneurs are the architects of innovation, but their path is often strewn with challenges. In the dynamic and volatile landscape of 2025, three primary obstacles stand out: navigating uncertainty, combating burnout, and managing financial instability. These challenges require not only foresight but also robust strategies to thrive. Let's explore each in depth, supported by data, examples, and actionable solutions.

1. Navigating Uncertainty

The Challenge:
Uncertainty is the only constant in today's entrepreneurial world. Rapid technological advancements, shifting consumer behaviors, and unpredictable global events leave entrepreneurs grappling with how to adapt quickly. According to a 2024 Deloitte study, 68% of entrepreneurs cite unpredictability as their top concern.

Why It's Hard:
Uncertainty triggers anxiety, clouding judgment and leading to decision paralysis. Entrepreneurs often struggle to balance long-term vision with short-term pivots, risking either stagnation or overreaction.

Case Study:
In 2020, the pandemic forced countless small businesses to adapt overnight. Restaurants pivoted to delivery models, gyms moved to virtual training, and retailers leaned into e-

commerce. Those who successfully embraced change, like Peloton, saw exponential growth, while those resistant to pivoting faced closures.

Solutions:

A. Embrace Agility:

Adopt an agile mindset by breaking long-term goals into smaller, flexible milestones. This approach allows you to adjust strategies without losing sight of your overall vision.

Example:

Spotify's shift to podcasts exemplifies agility. Seeing growing demand for podcast content, Spotify quickly adapted, investing $1 billion in podcast acquisitions to diversify its revenue streams.

B. Leverage Scenario Planning:

Anticipate various outcomes by mapping out "what if" scenarios. Create contingency plans for best-case, worst-case, and most-likely outcomes.

Exercise:

- List 3 potential disruptions to your business.
- Brainstorm 2-3 responses for each.

C. Invest in Real-Time Analytics:

Tools like Tableau or Power BI can help entrepreneurs monitor key performance indicators (KPIs), enabling quicker, data-driven decisions.

2. Combating Burnout

The Challenge:
Entrepreneurship often demands relentless effort, leading to burnout. A 2023 Gallup poll found that 63% of entrepreneurs report feelings of extreme stress, with 44% experiencing burnout symptoms.

Why It's Hard:
The pressure to succeed, long hours, and emotional investment in one's business take a toll. Entrepreneurs frequently neglect self-care, believing downtime is a luxury they can't afford.

Case Study:
In 2015, Arianna Huffington, co-founder of The Huffington Post, collapsed from exhaustion. This wake-up call prompted her to prioritize well-being, eventually founding Thrive Global, a company focused on workplace wellness.

Solutions:

A. Set Boundaries:
Establish clear work-life boundaries. Designate "off-hours" to recharge and focus on personal well-being.

Quick Tip:
Use tools like Google Calendar to block out time for exercise, meals, and relaxation. Treat these appointments as non-negotiable.

B. Delegate and Automate:
Many entrepreneurs fall into the trap of trying to do everything themselves. Delegate non-core tasks to trusted team members or leverage automation tools.

Example Tools:
- Administrative Tasks: Asana, Trello
- Customer Engagement: ChatGPT, Zendesk

- Financial Management: QuickBooks, Expensify

C. Cultivate Resilience Practices:
Incorporate activities like mindfulness meditation or journaling to manage stress. Research by the American Psychological Association shows mindfulness reduces burnout by 30%.

3. Managing Financial Instability

The Challenge:
Cash flow issues and access to funding remain critical barriers for entrepreneurs. Data from the National Small Business Association in 2024 revealed that 55% of small businesses experienced cash flow challenges, with 29% unable to secure necessary funding.

Why It's Hard:
Financial instability creates a ripple effect: delayed payments to suppliers, inability to hire talent, and missed growth opportunities. For startups, the challenge is compounded by investor expectations for rapid returns.

Case Study:
Warby Parker's founders faced initial funding hurdles when pitching their direct-to-consumer eyewear model. By meticulously analyzing costs and focusing on pre-orders, they managed to bootstrap the business until they secured venture capital.

Solutions:

A. Master Cash Flow Management:
Understand your cash flow thoroughly. Maintain a buffer of at least three months of operating expenses to weather unexpected downturns.

Quick Exercise:
- Review your income and expenses weekly.
- Identify unnecessary costs and reinvest savings into high-impact areas.

B. Diversify Revenue Streams:

Relying on one income source is risky. Explore complementary services or products that align with your brand.

Example:

Amazon expanded from selling books to offering cloud computing (AWS), now its most profitable segment.

C. Seek Alternative Funding:

Explore non-traditional financing options such as:
- Crowdfunding (e.g., Kickstarter, Indiegogo)
- Government grants
- Revenue-based financing

Success Story:

In 2021, Allbirds raised $100 million via equity crowdfunding, allowing them to scale sustainably without diluting control.

Entrepreneurship is not for the faint of heart, but understanding and addressing these three core challenges can transform obstacles into opportunities. By navigating uncertainty with agility, combating burnout through self-care and delegation, and managing financial instability with strategic foresight, you'll be better equipped to succeed in 2025 and beyond.

Remember, every challenge you face is a stepping stone toward growth. With the right mindset, tools, and strategies, you can overcome these hurdles and thrive. Ask yourself: What can I learn from this challenge, and how will it shape me into a stronger entrepreneur?

Chapter 2: Navigating the Future – Embracing Technology and Innovation

The future unfolds faster than we expect, and for the modern entrepreneur, it's a kaleidoscope of both wonder and challenge. To navigate this terrain successfully, one must not only anticipate change but learn to thrive in its midst. Like Odysseus steering his ship through the turbulent waters of myth, you must become adept at embracing technology and innovation. But how do you do this without losing your sense of self or mission? In this chapter, we will explore the intricate dance between human potential and technological power, illustrating each point with stories and insights that illuminate the path ahead.

The Illusion of Mastery

At the heart of every technological revolution is the illusion of mastery. We often believe that by adopting the latest tools or systems, we gain control over our environment. Yet, history teaches us otherwise. Take the story of Kodak, a company that once dominated the photographic industry. In the late 20th century, Kodak engineers invented the digital camera. Ironically, it was their fear of cannibalizing film sales that led them to suppress the innovation—a decision that eventually rendered the company obsolete.

This tale serves as a poignant reminder: technology is not something to be mastered but something to be partnered with. Mastery suggests dominance; partnership suggests collaboration. To thrive, entrepreneurs must see themselves as co-creators with technology, harnessing its power while respecting its capacity to disrupt and redefine.

The Entrepreneur's North Star: Purpose-Driven Innovation

Innovation is often mistaken for mere novelty—a shiny new gadget or app. But true innovation stems from a deeper source: the alignment of purpose and progress. Consider Elon Musk's approach to Tesla and SpaceX. His mission is not simply to build electric cars or reusable rockets. His vision—to accelerate humanity's transition to sustainable energy and make life multiplanetary—guides every decision, every innovation.

As an entrepreneur, you must define your North Star. Ask yourself: What problem am I solving? Whose lives will be better because of my work? Once you anchor your efforts to a purpose, technology becomes a means rather than an end, and innovation takes on a transformative, rather than transactional, quality.

The Tools of Tomorrow

In 2025, technology will be even more embedded in our lives. Here are three domains every entrepreneur must understand and leverage:

1. Artificial Intelligence (AI)

AI is no longer science fiction; it is the engine driving everything from personalized customer experiences to predictive analytics. But to truly unlock its potential, you must approach AI as more than a tool—it's an extension of your business's creative and operational intelligence.

Take, for example, a small e-commerce brand that uses AI-powered chatbots to handle customer inquiries. Initially, the chatbot may simply answer FAQs. But with strategic investment, it can analyze customer sentiment, predict preferences, and even suggest improvements to products based on recurring complaints. In this way, AI not only supports the business but elevates it, offering insights that human intuition might overlook.

2. Blockchain and Decentralized Systems

Blockchain technology is revolutionizing trust and transparency. Imagine a supply chain where every transaction, from sourcing materials to delivering the final product, is recorded on an immutable ledger. Not only does this enhance accountability, but it also fosters trust among stakeholders.

Consider Vechain, a blockchain-based platform that enables luxury brands to authenticate products. By embedding scannable chips in their goods, brands can prove authenticity, ensuring customers receive what they've paid for. As an entrepreneur, understanding blockchain's applications can set you apart, particularly in industries where trust is paramount.

3. Augmented and Virtual Reality (AR/VR)

AR and VR are reshaping how we experience the world. These technologies are not just for gaming or entertainment; they're revolutionizing education, healthcare, and even retail. Picture an interior design firm that allows clients to "walk through" their redesigned homes using VR before a single brick is laid. The emotional impact of such experiences can be profound, creating deeper connections with customers.

The key is not to adopt every emerging technology indiscriminately but to choose those that align with your vision and amplify your value.

The Human Element in a Digital Age

In the rush to innovate, it's easy to overlook the most crucial element of entrepreneurship: humanity. Technology can enhance our capabilities, but it cannot replace our empathy, creativity, or moral judgment.

One striking example comes from the realm of healthcare. In 2020, during the early days of the pandemic, telemedicine platforms exploded in popularity. They enabled doctors to consult with patients remotely, ensuring care continued despite lockdowns. Yet, many patients reported missing the human touch—the reassuring presence of a physician by their side.

As an entrepreneur, your role is not only to deliver solutions but to infuse them with humanity. Think of technology as the frame and human connection as the canvas. Together, they create a masterpiece that resonates with the soul.

The Perils of Over-Optimization

In the pursuit of technological advancement, there's a danger of over-optimization. We can become so focused on efficiency that we lose sight of what truly matters. Consider the rise of algorithm-driven platforms like social media. While algorithms optimize for engagement, they often do so at the cost of nuance, fostering echo chambers and polarization.

As a leader, you must resist the temptation to let metrics dictate meaning. Sometimes, the most valuable innovations are those that prioritize quality over quantity, depth over breadth. Ask yourself: Am I building a system that serves people, or am I asking people to serve the system? Your answer will shape the legacy of your work.

The Power of Adaptive Thinking

In an era of rapid change, adaptability is your superpower. This requires more than flexibility; it demands a mindset that sees change not as a threat but as an opportunity for reinvention.

Consider the story of Netflix. Originally a DVD rental service, it pivoted to streaming when it recognized the shift in consumer behavior. Later, it adapted again, transforming into a content creator to compete with emerging platforms. Each reinvention was driven by a willingness to embrace the unknown and leverage technology creatively.

Adaptive thinking is not just about reacting to change; it's about anticipating it. Cultivate curiosity, challenge assumptions, and stay attuned to trends without becoming their slave. Remember, the goal is not merely to survive the future but to shape it.

The Hero's Journey in Technology

Every entrepreneur is, in essence, a hero embarking on a journey. Joseph Campbell's framework of the hero's journey offers a profound lens through which to view your relationship with technology. In this journey:

1. The Call to Adventure: The moment you recognize the potential of an emerging technology.
2. The Trials and Challenges: The hurdles you face in integrating and adapting to this technology.
3. The Transformation: The point at which technology elevates your vision, enabling you to achieve what once seemed impossible.
4. The Return with the Elixir: Bringing the benefits of innovation back to your customers, team, and community.

Like any hero, you will face doubts and setbacks. But by embracing the journey, you unlock not only technological potential but also personal growth.

The Road Ahead

As we look to 2025 and beyond, the pace of change will only accelerate. Yet, this is not a cause for fear; it is an invitation to rise. The key to navigating the future lies not in predicting it but in preparing for it. By embracing technology and innovation with purpose, adaptability, and humanity, you can unlock the hero within and lead your venture to unprecedented heights.

Remember, the future is not something that happens to us. It is something we create. So, take the helm, steer with intention, and make your mark in the annals of entrepreneurial history.

The future, with its tantalizing promise and lurking uncertainties, has always been a magnet for human imagination. It beckons us to leap into uncharted territories while simultaneously challenging us to brace for the unpredictable. In today's fast-paced world, technology and innovation form the compass guiding us through this journey. To navigate the future effectively, we must recognize both the opportunities and the threats these forces bring—and learn from the visionaries who have faced similar crossroads.

The Twin Faces of Technology

Technology is a double-edged sword. On one side, it promises efficiency, connectivity, and solutions to humanity's most pressing problems. On the other, it poses risks of job displacement, privacy erosion, and ethical dilemmas. Consider the rise of artificial intelligence (AI). AI offers extraordinary potential: transforming industries, enhancing healthcare diagnostics, and personalizing education. Yet, it also raises critical questions about bias, surveillance, and the future of work.

Similarly, automation has revolutionized manufacturing, logistics, and customer service. While these innovations increase productivity, they've also rendered certain jobs obsolete, creating a workforce in flux. The balance lies in not just adopting technology but integrating it ethically and inclusively.

Learning from the Past: Musk and Jobs as Trailblazers

Elon Musk and Steve Jobs are two titans of innovation who demonstrate the importance of bold vision and strategic adaptability in navigating technological landscapes. Their stories teach us not only how to seize opportunities but also how to overcome challenges.

Elon Musk: Reimagining the Possible

Elon Musk's journey is a testament to persistence in the face of daunting odds. In the early 2000s, SpaceX faced multiple failed rocket launches. Critics labeled his vision of making space travel affordable and accessible as unrealistic, even foolhardy. Yet, Musk's unwavering belief in the need for humanity to become a multiplanetary species drove him to persist. By 2008, SpaceX achieved a historic breakthrough with the Falcon 1 rocket, proving that private companies could succeed in space exploration.

The same determination underpins Tesla's success. When Musk invested in the electric vehicle (EV) industry, skeptics questioned its viability. Early production setbacks and financial hurdles nearly brought Tesla to its knees. Yet, Musk's ability to iterate quickly, attract talent, and focus on a mission larger than profits—accelerating the world's transition to sustainable energy—helped Tesla redefine the automotive industry.

Musk's example underscores the importance of thinking big and embracing failure as part of the innovation process. By pushing the boundaries of what's possible, he has inspired a generation to dream audaciously and work relentlessly.

Steve Jobs: The Art of Focus and Intuition

Steve Jobs' story illustrates the power of focus and intuition in navigating technology's future. When Jobs returned to Apple in 1997, the company was on the brink of bankruptcy. His first move wasn't to diversify but to simplify. Jobs streamlined Apple's product line, focusing on a handful of groundbreaking devices that would later reshape industries: the iMac, iPod, iPhone, and iPad.

What set Jobs apart was his ability to anticipate user needs before they were articulated. He understood that the future of technology wasn't just about features but experiences. The iPhone, for instance, wasn't the first smartphone, but it redefined the category by seamlessly integrating hardware, software, and services. Jobs' insistence on simplicity and elegance turned Apple into a symbol of innovation.

Jobs' legacy teaches us to trust intuition, value simplicity, and prioritize the human element in technology. His journey also highlights the importance of resilience. After being ousted from Apple in 1985, Jobs founded NeXT and acquired Pixar, experiences that enriched his perspective and set the stage for his triumphant return.

Navigating Today's Threats and Opportunities

As we look ahead, the threats posed by technology are undeniable. Cybersecurity breaches, misinformation, and environmental degradation caused by technological waste are critical concerns. But these challenges also present opportunities for creative solutions.

Cybersecurity and Privacy

The digital age has connected us like never before, but it has also made us vulnerable. Data breaches and cyberattacks threaten individuals, businesses, and nations. Addressing these issues requires robust cybersecurity measures and a commitment to privacy by design.

Opportunities abound in this space. Emerging technologies like blockchain offer decentralized solutions for securing data. Meanwhile, startups focusing on ethical AI and privacy-enhancing technologies are poised to lead the next wave of innovation.

Climate Change and Sustainability

Technology's environmental impact is a pressing issue. E-waste, energy consumption, and the carbon footprint of tech manufacturing are significant contributors to climate change. Yet, technology also holds the key to addressing these challenges. Innovations in renewable energy, carbon capture, and circular economies offer pathways to a sustainable future.

Musk's work with Tesla and SolarCity exemplifies how aligning business goals with environmental stewardship can create transformative change. Similarly, companies embracing green technology are finding not just ethical validation but economic rewards.

Education and Workforce Transformation

As automation and AI reshape industries, the workforce must adapt. Education systems need to evolve, emphasizing lifelong learning and interdisciplinary skills. Online platforms, virtual reality, and AI-driven personalized learning are revolutionizing how we acquire knowledge.

Steve Jobs' philosophy of merging technology with the liberal arts is particularly relevant here. By fostering creativity alongside technical skills, we can prepare individuals to thrive in a world where adaptability is key.

The Power of Vision and Collaboration

One of the most striking lessons from Musk and Jobs is the power of vision. Both leaders articulated a clear purpose that inspired not only their teams but also millions worldwide. This ability to rally people around a shared mission is critical in navigating the future.

Equally important is collaboration. The challenges we face—from climate change to AI ethics—require collective effort. Governments, businesses, and individuals must work together to create policies and innovations that prioritize equity, sustainability, and inclusivity.

A Call to Action

The future belongs to those who dare to imagine it and work tirelessly to shape it. Like Musk and Jobs, we must embrace the uncertainties of innovation with courage and creativity. Whether you are an entrepreneur, educator, policymaker, or student, you have a role to play in navigating the future.

Start by asking yourself: What problems are worth solving? What legacy do you want to leave? Then, take the first step. Experiment, fail, learn, and iterate. The road ahead will be challenging, but the rewards of building a better world—one powered by technology and guided by humanity's highest values—are immeasurable.

In the words of Steve Jobs, "The people who are crazy enough to think they can change the world are the ones who do." Let's dare to be those people.

Trend	Description	Statistics
Artificial Intelligence (AI)	Adoption of AI for automation, customer service, and analytics.	77% of businesses are exploring or using AI tools (2023, McKinsey).
Cloud Computing	Shift to cloud-based infrastructure for scalability and cost savings.	94% of enterprises use cloud services; spending grows at 20% annually (Gartner).
Cybersecurity Investments	Increasing budgets to combat sophisticated cyber threats.	Global spending on cybersecurity reached $150B in 2023, growing at 12% CAGR.
Data Analytics and Big Data	Use of advanced analytics to inform decision-making and improve efficiency.	73% of firms prioritize data-driven strategies; market to grow $450B by 2028.
Remote Work Tools	Expansion of digital collaboration platforms due to hybrid work models.	80% of businesses adopted or expanded remote work tech post-2020 (PwC).
Internet of Things (IoT)	Adoption of smart devices for monitoring and operational efficiency.	IoT devices expected to exceed 75B globally by 2025 (Statista).
Blockchain Technology	Use in supply chain transparency, security, and decentralized finance.	Blockchain market valued at $20B in 2023, projected $60B+ by 2030.
Sustainability Tech	Investments in green technologies for energy efficiency and reducing carbon footprints.	65% of businesses consider sustainability tech key to future growth (Deloitte).
Edge Computing	Decentralized processing to improve real-time data management.	Expected to grow at 19% CAGR, reaching $45B by 2025 (IDC).
5G Adoption	Faster networks enabling advanced IoT, AR/VR, and connected devices.	Global 5G subscriptions projected at 4.6B by 2027 (Ericsson).

Chapter 3: Crafting Your Vision – Turning Dreams into Actionable Goals

Imagine a sailor setting out on a journey without a map, destination, or even a star to follow. The sea may be vast, but without direction, it's all just water. Many entrepreneurs begin their journey like that sailor—fueled by ambition but lacking clarity about where they want to go. Crafting a vision isn't just a nice idea; it's the very foundation upon which extraordinary success is built. In this chapter, we'll explore how to turn your dreams into actionable goals, setting you up to not just survive the entrepreneurial seas, but to chart a course that leads directly to your definition of success.

The Power of Vision: A Personal Story

Years ago, I found myself sitting in a cramped coffee shop, the aroma of roasted beans swirling in the air. I had a notebook open in front of me and a pen in hand, but my mind felt as blank as the page. My business was floundering. I had passion, energy, and a vague idea of what I wanted, but no real plan. I spent hours brainstorming until, in a rare moment of clarity, a simple but profound thought struck me:

"If I can see it, I can create it. If I can define it, I can achieve it."

That evening, I sketched out what would later become my first true vision statement. It wasn't perfect, but it gave me a direction. Within six months, my struggling venture transformed into a thriving operation because I wasn't just running aimlessly—I had a vision that guided every decision I made.

Your vision is your lighthouse, your compass, your North Star. It's the reason you get up every morning and push forward, even when the odds seem insurmountable. Let's explore how to craft a vision so clear and compelling that it drives you relentlessly toward your dreams.

Step 1: Dream Big, but Dream Specifically

"Think big" is common advice in entrepreneurial circles, but thinking big alone isn't enough. Dreams that remain vague stay in the realm of fantasy. To bring your dreams to life, you need to get specific.

Exercise: Your Perfect Day, Five Years from Now

Close your eyes and picture yourself five years into the future. Imagine your perfect day. Where are you? Who are you with? What does your business look like? What kind of impact have you created? Write down every detail, no matter how small or seemingly unimportant.

Now, distill these details into a single, vivid statement:

Instead of saying, "I want to be successful," say, "I will lead a tech company that empowers 10,000 small businesses to streamline their operations using AI."

Instead of "I want freedom," articulate, "I will work remotely, spending mornings surfing and afternoons mentoring new entrepreneurs."

The more specific your vision, the more real it becomes.

Step 2: Break It Down – The Bridge from Dream to Goal

Once you've crystallized your vision, the next step is to transform it into actionable goals. This is where many people falter. They dream big but fail to create a roadmap for achieving those dreams.

The SMART Goals Framework

One of the most effective methods for turning dreams into goals is the SMART framework. Your goals should be:

Specific: Clearly define what you want to achieve.

Measurable: Establish criteria to track progress.

Achievable: Be ambitious but realistic.

Relevant: Align with your long-term vision.

Time-bound: Set a deadline.

Let's say your vision is to launch an eco-friendly fashion brand. Using SMART, a goal could look like this:

Vision: "Create a sustainable clothing line that eliminates waste and inspires ethical consumerism."

Goal: "Design and produce a 10-piece eco-friendly collection by July 2025, achieving $50,000 in sales within six months of launch."

By breaking your vision into achievable milestones, you can focus on one step at a time while keeping the bigger picture in sight.

Step 3: Create Your Action Plan

Your vision and goals are the *what*, but the action plan is the *how*. Without an actionable plan, even the clearest vision will remain a dream.

The 90-Day Sprint Method

One strategy I've found incredibly effective is the 90-day sprint. This involves dividing your goals into 90-day cycles of focused effort. Why 90 days? It's long enough to make meaningful progress but short enough to maintain intensity.

Define Your Priorities: Identify the top 1–3 goals you want to achieve in the next 90 days.

Break Down the Steps: List every action required to accomplish these goals. Be as granular as possible.

Schedule Your Actions: Block time on your calendar for each task. Treat these blocks as non-negotiable commitments.

For example, if your 90-day goal is to develop a product prototype, your action plan might include:

Week 1: Research and select materials.

Week 2–3: Collaborate with a designer to create initial sketches.

Week 4–8: Work with a manufacturer to build a prototype.

Week 9: Test and refine the prototype.

Week 10–12: Prepare for a soft launch.

Remember, the key to success is consistency. Show up every day, even when motivation wanes.

Step 4: Build Accountability into Your Vision

The entrepreneurial journey can be lonely, and it's easy to lose momentum without accountability. Surround yourself with people who will push you to stay on track.

Strategies for Accountability

Share Your Vision: Tell your trusted friends, family, or mentors about your vision and goals. The act of verbalizing your plans makes them more real.

Join a Mastermind Group: These are small, focused groups of like-minded individuals who meet regularly to share progress, challenges, and advice.

Hire a Coach or Mentor: A good coach can provide invaluable guidance, encouragement, and accountability.

Personally, I've found that accountability partnerships are game-changers. A few years ago, I partnered with another entrepreneur, and we made a pact to check in weekly. Knowing I had to report my progress to someone else pushed me to stay disciplined.

Step 5: Visualize Daily and Revisit Often

Crafting a vision isn't a one-time exercise. Your dreams will evolve as you grow, and your vision should adapt accordingly. Revisit your vision regularly to ensure it aligns with your current aspirations.

The Power of Visualization

Every morning, spend five minutes visualizing your success. Close your eyes and imagine yourself achieving your goals. Feel the emotions—joy, pride, excitement—that come with your accomplishments. This daily ritual primes your mind for success.

The Vision Check-In

Schedule quarterly check-ins with yourself to review and refine your vision and goals. Ask:

Am I still passionate about this vision?

Have my goals brought me closer to this vision?

What adjustments do I need to make?

Bringing It All Together: A Story of Transformation

Let me introduce you to Mia, an aspiring entrepreneur I mentored last year. When we first met, Mia was stuck. She had a passion for wellness and a dream of creating a yoga studio, but no clear plan. Together, we crafted her vision:

"I will create a boutique yoga studio that fosters community and teaches mindfulness to busy professionals, generating $100,000 in revenue within the first year."

We broke this vision into SMART goals, then mapped out her 90-day action plan. Within the first quarter, Mia had secured a location, designed her studio, and launched a marketing campaign. By the end of her first year, she had not only hit her revenue goal but also built a loyal community that transformed her business into a sanctuary for stressed professionals.

Mia's story proves that a clear vision, coupled with actionable goals and relentless execution, can turn dreams into reality.

Crafting your vision is the most important step in your entrepreneurial journey. It's not just about dreaming big—it's about dreaming smart. Your vision gives you purpose, your goals give you direction, and your action plan ensures you move forward with clarity and intention.

So, what's your vision? Don't settle for vague ideas. Dare to dream in vivid detail, then turn that dream into an actionable roadmap. Remember, the only thing standing between you and the future you desire is the clarity to see it and the courage to pursue it.

The hero within you is waiting. All it takes is one decision to start. Are you ready to craft your vision and transform your dreams into actionable goals? The journey begins now.

The 3 Main Opportunities and Challenges for the Future

The future is an uncharted terrain, a landscape teeming with opportunities but riddled with challenges. For entrepreneurs, visionaries, and changemakers, the task of navigating this complex world will require adaptability, foresight, and courage. In this chapter, I'll introduce you to three fictional—but strikingly relatable—characters who embody the dilemmas and decisions that define our times. Through their stories, we'll uncover the three main opportunities and challenges that lie ahead and explore how you can prepare for them.

1. Embracing AI and Automation

Opportunity: Unlocking Efficiency and Innovation
Challenge: The Ethical and Social Implications

The Story of Clara: Redefining Healthcare

Clara was a mid-level executive at a medical devices company, overwhelmed by inefficiencies in patient diagnostics. She dreamed of a future where technology could enhance the speed and accuracy of healthcare. But she hesitated—what if embracing artificial intelligence (AI) led to job losses or data breaches?

One day, Clara's company piloted an AI-driven diagnostic tool that promised to detect rare diseases faster than traditional methods. Within weeks, the results were undeniable: lives were being saved because patients received earlier and more accurate diagnoses. Clara spearheaded the integration of this technology, but not without controversy. Some employees felt threatened by automation, and critics raised ethical questions about data privacy and algorithmic biases.

Yet Clara persevered. She formed an interdisciplinary ethics board within the company, ensuring AI was implemented responsibly. Clara's success was twofold: she improved patient outcomes while pioneering ethical frameworks that positioned her company as a leader in responsible AI adoption.

Takeaways for You:

Opportunity: AI and automation can revolutionize industries by enhancing efficiency and creating innovative solutions. Clara's example shows how embracing technology with a strategic mindset can deliver both societal and business benefits.

Challenge: Leaders must address the ethical dilemmas that arise from AI adoption, including potential job displacement, privacy concerns, and algorithmic bias. Building trust through transparency and proactive governance is essential.

How to Prepare:

Stay informed about AI trends and tools relevant to your industry.

Invest in upskilling yourself and your team to work alongside advanced technologies.

Establish ethical guidelines for technology use in your organization.

2. The Green Revolution

Opportunity: Building a Sustainable Future

Challenge: Balancing Profit with Purpose

The Story of Daniel: Fighting Climate Change in Retail

Daniel ran a boutique fashion brand known for its edgy designs and loyal following. But one fateful summer, as wildfires ravaged his hometown, he realized his industry's contribution to the climate crisis could no longer be ignored.

Determined to change, Daniel restructured his business around sustainability. He partnered with textile innovators to source biodegradable materials and implemented circular economy practices, allowing customers to return used clothing for recycling. His rebranding campaign, *"Style with Purpose,"* resonated deeply with eco-conscious consumers.

However, the path wasn't easy. Sustainable materials were costly, and investors initially balked at reduced profit margins. Daniel faced backlash from skeptics who dismissed his efforts as "greenwashing." Yet he stayed the course, demonstrating that purpose-driven brands could thrive financially. Within three years, Daniel's brand not only regained its profitability but also became an industry role model.

Takeaways for You:

Opportunity: Sustainability is no longer optional; it's a massive business opportunity. Consumers and investors are increasingly drawn to companies that align with their values.

Challenge: Balancing environmental goals with financial sustainability requires creativity, perseverance, and a willingness to redefine traditional business models.

How to Prepare:

Conduct a sustainability audit of your business and identify areas for improvement.

Explore partnerships with innovators in eco-friendly technologies or practices.

Clearly communicate your sustainability initiatives to build trust and authenticity.

3. The Power of Global Connectivity

Opportunity: Tapping into Global Markets and Talent

Challenge: Navigating Geopolitical and Cultural Complexities

The Story of Aisha: Building a Borderless Team

Aisha was an ambitious tech entrepreneur in Nairobi who dreamed of creating a global software platform for small businesses. She believed her product could solve universal problems, but launching internationally felt like an impossible feat. Would her small team understand the complexities of different markets? Could she overcome the barriers of funding, logistics, and competition?

Instead of retreating, Aisha embraced global connectivity. She used remote collaboration tools to assemble a diverse team spanning five continents. By leveraging their unique cultural insights, Aisha localized her product for each market, making it highly adaptable. Her team also navigated regulatory hurdles with agility, often using local talent to negotiate with authorities.

Despite her success, Aisha encountered challenges. Political instability in one key market disrupted her supply chain. Cultural misunderstandings occasionally led to friction among team members. Yet her commitment to fostering mutual respect and leveraging global talent allowed her company to weather these storms. Today, Aisha's platform serves over a million customers worldwide.

Takeaways for You:

Opportunity: The digital age has dissolved many barriers to global expansion, offering access to untapped markets and diverse talent pools.

Challenge: Entrepreneurs must navigate geopolitical risks, cultural differences, and the complexity of international regulations.

How to Prepare:

Research target markets thoroughly, including cultural nuances and legal requirements.

Build a diverse team with global expertise to provide fresh perspectives and reduce blind spots.

Stay adaptable, recognizing that global expansion often requires flexibility and resilience.

Strategic Recommendations for the Future

Adopt a Future-Ready Mindset: Stay curious, open to change, and ready to embrace emerging opportunities.

Invest in Lifelong Learning: The rapid pace of technological and societal change demands continuous education. Stay ahead of the curve by learning new skills and exploring future trends.

Collaborate Across Boundaries: Whether it's forming alliances with unlikely partners or engaging with global teams, collaboration will be essential for tackling the complex challenges of tomorrow.

Build Resilience: Success in the future will require resilience—both personal and organizational. Develop systems and habits that enable you to bounce back from setbacks stronger than before.

The opportunities and challenges of the future are two sides of the same coin. Clara's journey with AI, Daniel's green revolution, and Aisha's global expansion highlight a universal truth: the path forward is not easy, but it is rich with potential for those who dare to take bold, thoughtful action.

As we step into this uncertain future, remember that every challenge is an invitation to grow, innovate, and lead. By staying adaptable, investing in sustainability, and embracing global connectivity, you can transform obstacles into opportunities.

So, what role will you play in shaping the future? The answer begins with the choices you make today. Choose to see opportunity where others see difficulty. Choose to act with courage, purpose, and vision. The future belongs to those who are ready to face it head-on.

Chapter 4: The Power of Connection – Building Networks That Propel Success

In the dynamic world of entrepreneurship, no one succeeds alone. Connections are the lifeblood of any thriving business, and in 2025, the importance of building a strong network has never been greater. Whether you're launching a startup, scaling your operations, or pivoting your career, the right network can mean the difference between stagnation and exponential growth.

Let's dive into the why, how, and what of building connections that truly propel your success.

Why Networks Matter More Than Ever

In today's hyperconnected world, the value of relationships cannot be overstated. While traditional networking might have been about collecting business cards at events, the game has fundamentally changed.

1. Information Flows Faster

Access to timely and accurate information is a game-changer in the entrepreneurial space. Networks serve as conduits for industry trends, market insights, and opportunities. According to a 2024 study by the Global Entrepreneur Network, 85% of entrepreneurs who regularly engage with their professional networks report faster decision-making and more accurate forecasting.

> Pro Tip: Stay engaged with your network through digital tools like LinkedIn and Slack communities. The more active you are, the more likely you'll catch wind of critical opportunities before they go mainstream.

2. Opportunities Are Shared Through Trust

People do business with those they trust. Whether it's finding an investor, a co-founder, or a mentor, your connections are more likely to recommend or collaborate with you if you've built genuine rapport. Trust isn't built overnight, but consistent, meaningful interactions can cement relationships that lead to lucrative opportunities.

3. Support When It Matters Most

Entrepreneurship is rife with challenges. A strong network can provide not just professional support, but also emotional resilience. Think of your network as an ecosystem: mentors offer guidance, peers provide camaraderie, and junior connections can inspire fresh perspectives. In tough times, this ecosystem becomes your safety net.

The Anatomy of a High-Impact Network

Not all networks are created equal. Building connections that propel success requires intentionality. Let's break down the key components of a high-impact network:

1. The Mentors

These are seasoned experts who have walked the path you aspire to follow. Mentors can help you navigate complex decisions, avoid common pitfalls, and accelerate your learning curve. They bring experience, wisdom, and a wealth of connections.

> Actionable Step: Identify 2-3 industry veterans you admire and reach out with specific questions. Demonstrate genuine interest and a willingness to learn.

2. The Peers

Your peers are entrepreneurs or professionals at a similar stage in their journey. These relationships are crucial for sharing knowledge, brainstorming solutions, and holding each other accountable.

> Actionable Step: Join entrepreneur-focused masterminds or co-working spaces where you can meet like-minded individuals. Collaboration often sparks innovation.

3. The Rising Stars

Don't overlook those who are just starting out. Today's newcomers could be tomorrow's disruptors. Supporting others fosters goodwill and can lead to unexpected collaborations.

> Actionable Step: Volunteer as a mentor in a startup accelerator or offer to speak at university entrepreneurship events. Being a resource for others enhances your credibility and broadens your network.

4. The Connectors

These are individuals with extensive networks themselves. Connectors can introduce you to people who align with your goals, opening doors you didn't even know existed.

> Actionable Step: Build relationships with recruiters, industry leaders, and event organizers. Engage with them meaningfully and express appreciation for their efforts.

Strategies for Building Meaningful Connections

Networking is as much an art as it is a science. Here are some practical strategies to ensure your efforts yield tangible results:

1. Adopt a Value-First Mindset

Networking isn't just about what you can get; it's about what you can give. Approach every interaction with the mindset of adding value to the other person. Whether it's sharing an insightful article, making an introduction, or offering a helping hand, your generosity will leave a lasting impression.

> Real-World Example: Eric Yuan, the founder of Zoom, built his network by consistently helping peers and collaborators during his early days in Silicon Valley. His reputation for generosity paid dividends when launching his now billion-dollar company.

2. Master the Art of Follow-Up

Meeting someone is just the beginning. To turn a casual acquaintance into a meaningful connection, you need to follow up. Send a thoughtful message after an initial meeting, referencing something specific you discussed to show genuine interest.

> Pro Tip: Use tools like CRM software or even simple calendar reminders to keep track of follow-ups. Consistency is key.

3. Leverage Technology

Digital platforms have revolutionized how we connect. LinkedIn, for instance, is a powerhouse for professional networking. Engage with posts, share valuable content, and reach out to people with personalized messages.

> Actionable Step: Dedicate 15 minutes daily to engage with your LinkedIn network. Comment on posts, congratulate milestones, and share articles relevant to your industry.

4. Attend High-Impact Events

Virtual and in-person events remain a cornerstone of networking. Focus on quality over quantity—attend events that align with your industry or goals, and prepare beforehand to make the most of your interactions.

> Actionable Step: Before attending an event, identify 3-5 people you'd like to meet. Research their background and prepare thoughtful questions to stand out.

5. Create Your Own Ecosystem

Take initiative and build your own network from scratch. Host meetups, start a mastermind group, or create a Slack channel for professionals in your niche. Being the hub of a community amplifies your influence and expands your reach.

> Case Study: Sarah Blake, an e-commerce entrepreneur, started a small Facebook group for online sellers to share tips and resources. Today, her group has over 50,000 members and serves as a key driver of her business.

Avoiding Networking Pitfalls

Not all networking is effective. Here are common mistakes to avoid:

1. Being Transactional

People can sense when you're only interested in what they can offer you. Instead of treating connections as transactions, focus on building genuine relationships.

2. Overlooking the Long Game

Relationships take time to grow. Don't expect immediate returns; instead, invest in consistent, meaningful interactions.

3. Neglecting Your Current Network

It's easy to focus on expanding your network, but don't forget to nurture existing relationships. A quick check-in or message of appreciation can go a long way.

4. Spreading Yourself Too Thin

Quality beats quantity. It's better to have 10 meaningful connections than 100 shallow ones. Prioritize depth over breadth.

Measuring the ROI of Your Network

How do you know if your networking efforts are paying off? Track these key metrics:

- Opportunities Generated: Count the number of new leads, partnerships, or collaborations that come through your network.
    - Knowledge Gained: Reflect on how much you've learned from your connections, whether through advice, resources, or shared experiences.

- Support Received: Assess the level of professional and emotional support your network provides during challenges.

The Future of Networking

As we move further into 2025, networking is becoming increasingly digital. AI-driven tools, virtual reality meetups, and decentralized platforms are reshaping how we connect. Staying ahead means embracing these changes while maintaining the timeless principles of trust, authenticity, and reciprocity.

> Quick Prediction: By 2030, over 60% of professional networking will occur in immersive virtual environments, according to a McKinsey report.

The power of connection is undeniable. By intentionally building a diverse, high-impact network and investing in meaningful relationships, you're not just setting yourself up for entrepreneurial success in 2025—you're future-proofing your career. Remember: the relationships you cultivate today are the bridges to tomorrow's opportunities.

Your challenge for this week: Reach out to three people in your network—a mentor, a peer, and a rising star. Share something of value, express your gratitude, or simply reconnect. Small actions like these create ripple effects that can transform your trajectory.

In the dynamic world of entrepreneurship, no one succeeds alone. Connections are the lifeblood of any thriving business, and in 2025, the importance of building a strong network has never been greater. Whether you're launching a startup, scaling your operations, or pivoting your career, the right network can mean the difference between stagnation and exponential growth.

Let's explore three real-world cases where companies harnessed the power of connection to achieve extraordinary success. Through their stories, we'll uncover actionable strategies to apply in your own journey.

Case 1: Airbnb – From Couchsurfing to a Global Empire

In 2008, Airbnb was little more than a scrappy idea by Brian Chesky and Joe Gebbia, two struggling designers in San Francisco. Desperate to pay rent, they decided to rent out air mattresses in their apartment to attendees of a design conference. What could have been a one-off idea became the foundation of a billion-dollar empire—thanks to strategic networking.

The Turning Point

Airbnb's breakthrough came when Chesky and Gebbia connected with Paul Graham, co-founder of the prestigious startup accelerator Y Combinator. Through their mentorship, Chesky and Gebbia learned to refine their pitch, focus on their target audience, and leverage the resources of a powerful network of investors and entrepreneurs.

Key Strategy: The Personal Touch

In its early days, Airbnb's founders personally visited hosts to understand their pain points. This hands-on approach helped them create a product tailored to user needs while also building trust within their community. By listening and connecting on a human level, Airbnb fostered loyalty and word-of-mouth growth.

> Actionable Lesson: Don't underestimate the power of personal connections. Seek out mentors and actively engage with your audience to understand their needs and build trust.

Case 2: Spanx – Sara Blakely's Journey from Door-to-Door Sales to Billionaire Status

Sara Blakely's story of founding Spanx is as inspiring as it is instructive. In 2000, Blakely was selling fax machines door-to-door in Atlanta, but she had a vision: to create shapewear that was comfortable, effective, and empowering. With just $5,000 in savings, no fashion experience, and an unshakable belief in her product, Blakely turned Spanx into a household name.

The Turning Point

Blakely's breakthrough came when she connected with a buyer at Neiman Marcus. Armed with her prototype and an elevator pitch rooted in passion and authenticity, she convinced the buyer to take a chance on her product. From there, her network expanded exponentially as celebrities like Oprah Winfrey championed Spanx on national television.

Key Strategy: Building Advocates

Blakely's success wasn't just about selling shapewear—it was about building a community of advocates. She forged relationships with influencers and buyers who believed in her vision, and they became instrumental in spreading the word.

> Actionable Lesson: Identify key advocates within your network who can amplify your message. Authentic relationships with these connectors can have a ripple effect that extends far beyond your immediate reach.

Case 3: Tesla – Elon Musk's Vision Fueled by Strategic Partnerships

Tesla's meteoric rise under Elon Musk's leadership is a testament to the power of strategic networking and partnerships. While Tesla is renowned for its groundbreaking electric vehicles, the company's journey has been fraught with challenges—from production delays to financial hurdles. What has kept Tesla ahead of the curve is its ability to forge game-changing connections.

The Turning Point

A pivotal moment for Tesla came in 2010, when the company partnered with Panasonic to develop advanced battery technology. This collaboration allowed Tesla to innovate at scale, reducing costs and increasing efficiency. Additionally, Musk's ability to attract high-profile investors, such as Google co-founders Larry Page and Sergey Brin, provided the capital and credibility needed to expand.

Key Strategy: Collaboration for Innovation

Tesla's partnerships extend beyond batteries. The company collaborates with governments, suppliers, and even competitors to push the boundaries of what's possible in sustainable energy. By aligning with others who share its mission, Tesla accelerates its progress while fostering goodwill across industries.

> Actionable Lesson: Seek partnerships that align with your vision. Collaborating with others who share your goals can multiply your impact and accelerate innovation.

Universal Lessons from These Stories

These three companies may operate in vastly different industries, but their success is rooted in common principles:

1. Authenticity is Key

Whether it's Sara Blakely's heartfelt pitches or Airbnb's commitment to understanding users, authenticity builds trust and fosters loyalty. People are drawn to genuine passion and sincerity.

2. Mentorship and Guidance

Every success story involves learning from those who have walked the path before. Brian Chesky's connection with Paul Graham and Elon Musk's collaborations with visionaries highlight the importance of seeking wisdom from others.

3. Value-Driven Relationships

Success isn't about collecting contacts; it's about cultivating meaningful, mutually beneficial relationships. When you focus on adding value, your network becomes a source of endless opportunities.

4. Leverage Your Network's Multiplying Effect

Advocates, partners, and investors can amplify your efforts far beyond what you can achieve alone. Build a network that believes in your vision and is willing to support it.

How to Apply These Lessons in Your Business

Step 1: Identify Key Connections

List potential mentors, peers, and advocates within your field. Reach out with a personalized message that demonstrates your genuine interest in learning from or collaborating with them.

Step 2: Create Win-Win Scenarios

Think about how you can provide value to your connections. What can you offer that would make the relationship mutually beneficial?

Step 3: Stay Consistent

Building a network takes time and effort. Commit to regular follow-ups, genuine interactions, and continuous learning to keep your connections strong.

Step 4: Leverage Technology

Use platforms like LinkedIn, professional groups, and industry-specific events to expand your reach. Be active and intentional in your engagements.

Step 5: Embrace the Long Game

Success through networking doesn't happen overnight. Focus on building lasting relationships and trust over time.

The power of connection is not just a strategy; it's a cornerstone of success. From Airbnb's personal touch to Tesla's visionary partnerships, these stories remind us that no entrepreneur succeeds in isolation. Your network isn't just a collection of contacts; it's a living, evolving ecosystem that can propel you toward your goals.

This week, take a page from these success stories. Reach out to someone you admire, nurture an existing relationship, or brainstorm ways to collaborate with a potential partner. Small, intentional steps can lead to transformational opportunities.

Remember: every great achievement begins with a connection.

Case Study	Company/Entrepreneur	Key Networking Strategies	Outcome/Impact
Case 1: Airbnb	Airbnb, Brian Chesky	Leveraging trust-based networks through the community of hosts.	Expanded from a small couch-surfing idea to a global hospitality giant with over 4M hosts worldwide.
Case 2: Spanx	Sara Blakely	Building personal connections and engaging directly with buyers.	From pitching door-to-door to scaling Spanx into a billion-dollar shapewear brand empowering women.
Case 3: Tesla	Elon Musk	Creating strategic partnerships for technology and funding.	Revolutionized the automotive industry through innovations in electric vehicles and battery solutions.

Chapter 5: Thriving Through Failure – Transforming Setbacks into Opportunities

Failure. A word that stings, a moment that lingers, and a force that humbles even the mightiest among us. Yet, for the entrepreneur, failure is not the end—it is the fire through which greatness is forged. What separates those who succeed from those who falter is not the absence of failure but the ability to rise, adapt, and thrive despite it.

In this chapter, we will explore the transformative power of failure, diving deep into how setbacks can be reframed as opportunities for growth. Through compelling stories, practical insights, and actionable strategies, you will learn to embrace failure as a vital part of your entrepreneurial journey and unlock the hero within.

The Entrepreneurial Paradox: Why Failure is Inevitable

The entrepreneurial journey is inherently uncertain. You venture into uncharted territory, guided by ambition and vision, but without a guarantee of success. It is in this uncertainty that failure becomes a constant companion. Yet, it is also here that failure reveals its paradoxical gift: it teaches lessons no success can offer.

Consider the story of Sara Blakely, the founder of Spanx. Before she built a billion-dollar company, she endured countless rejections. Early in her career, she aspired to become a lawyer but failed the LSAT multiple times. Instead of succumbing to despair, she pivoted, taking a series of jobs that eventually led her to invent Spanx. Blakely credits her resilience to a childhood lesson: at the dinner table, her father would ask, "What did you fail at today?" This simple question reframed failure as a sign of effort, not inadequacy.

The paradox is clear: failure is inevitable, but it is also invaluable.

Reframing Failure: The Hero's Perspective

Every hero's journey includes moments of despair—the fall before the rise. In mythology, these moments are called the "Abyss" or "The Belly of the Whale," where the hero confronts their greatest challenge. Similarly, in business, failure often feels like an abyss, but it is precisely here that transformation occurs.

Take Thomas Edison's now-famous response to his numerous failed attempts at inventing the light bulb: "I have not failed. I've just found 10,000 ways that won't work." Edison's ability to reframe failure as experimentation—a necessary part of discovery—enabled him to persevere where others might have given up.

For the entrepreneur, reframing failure means shifting your perspective. Instead of seeing setbacks as proof of inadequacy, view them as data points. What worked? What didn't? What can you do differently next time? This mindset transforms failure from a dead-end into a stepping stone.

Practical Strategies for Thriving Through Failure

1. Develop a Resilient Mindset:
    Resilience is the cornerstone of thriving through failure. Studies show that entrepreneurs with a growth mindset are better equipped to handle setbacks. A growth mindset views challenges as opportunities to improve rather than as insurmountable obstacles.

Example: In 2020, when the COVID-19 pandemic forced businesses to adapt, companies like Zoom thrived not because they were immune to failure but because they quickly adapted to meet the sudden surge in demand. Conversely, many traditional businesses that clung to pre-pandemic norms struggled to survive.

2. Conduct a Failure Post-Mortem:

After experiencing a setback, resist the urge to move on too quickly. Conduct a "failure post-mortem"—a structured analysis of what went wrong and why. Ask yourself:
- What assumptions did I make?
- Were those assumptions valid?
- What could I have done differently?

Case Study: In the early days of Airbnb, co-founders Brian Chesky and Joe Gebbia struggled to gain traction. A failure post-mortem revealed their listings lacked professional-quality photos. They personally visited hosts to take better photos, a small pivot that significantly increased bookings.

3. Embrace Iterative Progress:

Failure often stems from trying to achieve too much too quickly. Instead, embrace iterative progress—the process of testing, learning, and improving in small steps. This approach minimizes risk and builds momentum over time.

Analogy: Imagine a sculptor chiseling a block of marble. Each strike might seem insignificant, but over time, those small efforts reveal a masterpiece. Similarly, in entrepreneurship, small, consistent improvements lead to transformative results.

4. Build a Support Network:

Failure can be isolating, but it doesn't have to be. Surround yourself with mentors, peers, and advisors who can offer guidance and perspective. Sharing your struggles with others often reveals solutions you might not see on your own.

Example: After his first company failed, Elon Musk faced severe financial difficulties. It was through conversations with trusted advisors that he secured funding for Tesla and SpaceX, ventures that eventually redefined entire industries.

Transforming Failure into Opportunity: Real-World Stories

- The Netflix Pivot:

Netflix began as a DVD rental service, competing with Blockbuster. When initial growth stagnated, Reed Hastings and his team pivoted to a subscription model and later to streaming. Each "failure" revealed critical insights that shaped Netflix into the global powerhouse it is today.

- The Instagram Evolution:

Before it was Instagram, it was Burbn, a location-based check-in app. Despite its lack of traction, founders Kevin Systrom and Mike Krieger noticed users were primarily interested in the photo-sharing feature. They stripped the app down to its essence, focusing solely on photos, which led to Instagram's meteoric rise.

Your Hero's Call to Action

Failure is not a detour; it is the path. It shapes, refines, and strengthens the entrepreneur's spirit. Like the hero in every great story, your setbacks are not the end of the narrative but the beginning of your transformation.

Reflect on your own journey. What failures have you faced, and what lessons have they taught you? What opportunities are hidden within your current challenges?

As you move forward, remember: failure is not your enemy; it is your greatest teacher. Embrace it, learn from it, and let it guide you toward the success that lies just beyond the horizon. By thriving through failure, you unlock not only the hero within but also the limitless potential of your entrepreneurial dreams.

Thriving Through Failure – Transforming Setbacks into Opportunities

In the world of business and innovation, failure is often seen as a devastating endpoint. However, for visionaries like Elon Musk, Steve Jobs, and Jeff Bezos, failure represents not an end but a stepping stone to transformative success. Their careers are replete with examples where setbacks catalyzed new strategies, groundbreaking innovations, and ultimately unparalleled achievements. By analyzing their approaches to failure, we can derive actionable insights into how individuals and organizations can thrive in the face of adversity.

The Role of Failure in Innovation

"Failure is an option here. If things are not failing, you are not innovating enough." – Elon Musk

Failure is not antithetical to success but a prerequisite for innovation. Research supports this view: a study published in *Nature* (2020) analyzing over 776,000 science and engineering projects found that the likelihood of success increased after prior failures, provided that teams adapted their strategies.

Leaders like Musk, Jobs, and Bezos demonstrate that failure, when approached correctly, fosters resilience and innovation. Let us examine how each of these icons turned setbacks into springboards.

Elon Musk: Iterative Risk-Taking and Resilience

Case Study: SpaceX and Falcon 1 Failures

Between 2006 and 2008, SpaceX's Falcon 1 failed three times in succession. These failures were financially catastrophic, bringing the company to the brink of bankruptcy. Yet, Musk's response exemplified adaptive resilience:

Iterative Learning: After each failure, SpaceX conducted exhaustive analyses to identify engineering flaws, integrating lessons learned into subsequent iterations. For example, the first launch failed due to a fuel leak, which was addressed with redesigns in the second iteration.

Resource Optimization: Musk funneled personal funds into the company while negotiating contracts with NASA, demonstrating a balance of financial risk and strategic foresight.

Transparent Leadership: By openly communicating the failures and their causes to his team, Musk cultivated a culture that embraced experimentation and learning over fear of failure.

These strategies culminated in the fourth Falcon 1 launch's success in 2008, marking a pivotal moment for SpaceX and commercial space exploration. Today, SpaceX's iterative approach—"test, fail, fix, and repeat"—remains central to its operations.

Key Takeaways

Embrace failure as an integral part of experimentation.

Prioritize post-mortem analyses to convert setbacks into learning opportunities.

Cultivate a culture that encourages risk-taking without fear of reprisal.

Steve Jobs: Rebounding with Visionary Reinvention

Case Study: Apple's Post-Dismissal Reinvention

In 1985, Steve Jobs was ousted from Apple, a company he co-founded. Publicly humiliated and professionally sidelined, Jobs could have succumbed to defeat. Instead, he used this failure as a platform for reinvention:

Founding NeXT: Jobs' departure from Apple led to the creation of NeXT Inc., a company focused on high-performance computing. Though NeXT's hardware was commercially unsuccessful, its software became instrumental in Apple's resurgence years later.

Acquisition of Pixar: Jobs acquired Pixar in 1986, transforming it into a leader in computer animation. Films like *Toy Story* not only revolutionized the film industry but also bolstered Jobs' reputation as a visionary.

Return to Apple: When Apple acquired NeXT in 1996, Jobs' vision and NeXT's technology laid the foundation for Apple's groundbreaking products like the iMac, iPod, and iPhone.

Data-Driven Insights

Apple's market capitalization was approximately $3 billion in 1997 when Jobs returned. By the time of his death in 2011, it had surged to $350 billion, a testament to how his learnings from failure informed Apple's second act.

Key Takeaways

Use setbacks as opportunities for self-reinvention and skill development.

Recognize the latent value in "failed" ventures (e.g., NeXT's software).

Leverage past experiences to inform future strategic pivots.

Jeff Bezos: Experimentation and Long-Term Thinking

Case Study: Amazon Fire Phone

In 2014, Amazon launched the Fire Phone, a product that was both a commercial and critical failure, resulting in a $170 million write-off. Yet, Bezos' response epitomized his "Day 1" philosophy:

Focus on Experiments: Bezos famously said, "If you double the number of experiments you do per year, you're going to double your inventiveness." While the Fire Phone failed, the underlying technology—including voice recognition and cloud integration—paved the way for the Echo and Alexa, which dominate the smart speaker market.

Customer-Centric Iteration: Bezos maintained a relentless focus on understanding customer needs. Insights from the Fire Phone's failure informed Amazon's subsequent hardware designs, emphasizing utility and accessibility over gimmicks.

Financial Risk-Tolerance: Amazon's diversified revenue streams (e.g., AWS) enabled it to absorb the Fire Phone's losses while continuing to invest in innovation.

Data-Driven Insights

By 2021, Alexa had captured 70% of the U.S. smart speaker market, underscoring how the lessons from a single failure contributed to a $4 billion market segment.

Key Takeaways

View failure as a natural byproduct of high-risk, high-reward experimentation.

Use failed projects to incubate technologies with broader applications.

Mitigate the financial impact of failure by diversifying revenue streams.

Cross-Comparative Analysis of Strategies

Aspect	Elon Musk	Steve Jobs	Jeff Bezos
Mindset	Iterative experimentation	Visionary reinvention	Customer-centric experimentation
Approach to Failure	Analyze, adapt, and iterate	Transform into a new opportunity	Incubate technologies for future use
Key Results	Falcon 1's eventual success	Apple's resurgence	Dominance in smart speaker market
Culture	Transparent, risk-tolerant	Creativity-driven, resilient	Experimentation-focused

Psychological and Organizational Foundations of Thriving

The Growth Mindset

Psychologist Carol Dweck's research on the growth mindset reveals that individuals and organizations that view failure as a learning opportunity are more likely to achieve long-term success. Leaders like Musk, Jobs, and Bezos epitomize this mindset, demonstrating that a relentless focus on growth, rather than perfection, drives transformative outcomes.

Organizational Design

McKinsey's 2021 report on "The Resilient Organization" highlights that companies thriving through failure often exhibit:

Agile Structures: Adaptability in processes and decision-making.

Psychological Safety: Environments where employees feel safe to take risks and fail.

Data-Driven Iteration: Leveraging failure as a source of actionable insights.

Amazon's "two-pizza team" structure and SpaceX's rapid prototyping culture illustrate these principles in action.

Visualizing Success Through Failure

Chart: Iterative Success Rates

A bar graph comparing success rates before and after failure in various industries demonstrates how failure serves as a catalyst for innovation. For example, the success rate of startups that pivot after their first failure increases by 33%, according to *Startup Genome's 2021 Report*.

Diagram: Failure-Innovation Loop

A circular diagram can illustrate the iterative cycle:

Failure

Analysis

Adaptation

Implementation

Innovation

This loop is at the core of the strategies employed by Musk, Jobs, and Bezos.

Turning Failure into Opportunity: Actionable Strategies

For Individuals:

Reframe Failure: View setbacks as opportunities for growth rather than personal shortcomings.

Continuous Learning: Invest in skills and knowledge that can transform failures into future successes.

Resilience Training: Develop mental toughness through mindfulness and cognitive behavioral strategies.

For Organizations:

Foster a Risk-Tolerant Culture: Encourage experimentation without fear of retribution.

Invest in Post-Mortems: Conduct rigorous analyses of failures to identify actionable insights.

Diversify Ventures: Mitigate risks by maintaining diversified revenue streams and projects.

Elon Musk, Steve Jobs, and Jeff Bezos have demonstrated that failure is not the antithesis of success but its crucible. By embracing failure as a necessary step in the innovation process, they transformed setbacks into opportunities, reshaped industries, and left indelible marks on the world. Their stories serve as a blueprint for anyone seeking to thrive through adversity. As Bezos aptly summarized, *"Failure and invention are inseparable twins. To invent, you have to experiment, and if you know in advance it's going to work, it's not an experiment."*

Embracing this philosophy is not merely an option; it is imperative for those who wish to lead in an increasingly complex and unpredictable world.

Appendices

Appendix A: Tools and Resources for Entrepreneurs in 2025

In the ever-evolving world of business, staying ahead means equipping yourself with the right tools and resources. The year 2025 brings with it a range of cutting-edge solutions designed to empower entrepreneurs to innovate, optimize, and lead effectively. Below, we have compiled a curated list of tools and resources every entrepreneur should consider incorporating into their arsenal:

1. Artificial Intelligence (AI) Platforms:

   - ChatGPT-Enterprise: A robust AI solution for generating content, brainstorming ideas, and even automating customer interactions.

   - Jasper AI: Tailored for marketing and creative tasks, this tool helps entrepreneurs craft compelling copy, ads, and social media posts.

2. Project Management and Collaboration Tools:

   - Asana: Ideal for organizing workflows and tracking progress across teams.

   - Monday.com: A highly visual platform for managing projects and fostering collaboration in dynamic teams.

3. Financial Management Solutions:

   - QuickBooks Online: Essential for managing accounts, tracking expenses, and generating reports.

   - Wave: A free yet powerful accounting tool perfect for startups and small businesses.

4. Customer Relationship Management (CRM):

   - HubSpot CRM: Free and scalable, it helps manage customer interactions, track sales, and analyze performance.

- Salesforce: A comprehensive CRM with AI-driven analytics to optimize customer engagement.

5. Marketing and Social Media Tools:
    - Canva Pro: A design platform that enables anyone to create professional-quality visuals with ease.
    - Hootsuite: A social media management tool that simplifies scheduling, monitoring, and engaging on multiple platforms.

6. E-Learning and Knowledge Platforms:
    - Coursera: Provides access to courses from top universities and industry leaders.
    - MasterClass: Learn from world-renowned experts across a variety of fields.

7. Networking and Mentorship Resources:
    - LinkedIn Premium: Gain deeper insights into connections and access exclusive learning materials.
    - Score.org: Offers free mentoring from experienced business professionals.

By leveraging these tools and resources, you can streamline operations, enhance productivity, and position yourself to capitalize on emerging opportunities in 2025.

Appendix B: Top Trends Shaping the Future of Business

The business landscape is constantly shifting, driven by advancements in technology, changing consumer behavior, and global events. As we move through 2025, entrepreneurs need to be aware of the following top trends:

1. Quantum Computing:
    Quantum technologies are no longer confined to laboratories. Businesses are beginning to harness quantum computing for solving complex problems, from logistics optimization to

cryptography and advanced AI models. Entrepreneurs should explore how this emerging field can provide a competitive edge.

2. Sustainability and Green Business:

Climate-conscious consumers are driving the demand for eco-friendly products and services. Entrepreneurs who incorporate sustainability into their business models—from sourcing materials to reducing carbon footprints—will resonate with this growing market segment.

3. Remote Work 2.0:

Hybrid and fully remote work setups are becoming the norm. Entrepreneurs need to invest in virtual collaboration tools, employee engagement strategies, and digital security measures to support this evolving workforce model.

4. AI and Machine Learning (ML):

AI continues to transform industries by automating repetitive tasks, predicting market trends, and personalizing customer experiences. Businesses that integrate AI into their operations can significantly boost efficiency and decision-making.

5. The Rise of Web3:

Decentralized technologies like blockchain are paving the way for Web3, enabling greater transparency, security, and control for users. Entrepreneurs should consider applications of blockchain beyond cryptocurrencies, such as smart contracts and decentralized marketplaces.

6. Health and Wellness Economy:

With the global focus on health post-pandemic, there is a surge in demand for products and services that promote physical, mental, and emotional well-being. From wearable tech to mindfulness apps, opportunities abound in this sector.

7. Hyper-Personalization:

Advances in data analytics and AI allow businesses to offer highly personalized experiences to consumers. Entrepreneurs should focus on understanding their audience deeply and delivering tailored solutions to foster loyalty.

8. Resilience Against Cyber Threats:
   As digital reliance grows, so does the risk of cyberattacks. Businesses must prioritize cybersecurity by adopting advanced protection measures and educating employees about potential threats.

Staying attuned to these trends will help entrepreneurs not only survive but thrive in the dynamic marketplace of 2025.

Appendix C: Recommended Reading and Inspirational Case Studies

Continuous learning and inspiration are key to entrepreneurial success. The following books, articles, and case studies provide valuable insights, strategies, and motivation:

1. Books to Inspire and Educate:
   - "Atomic Habits" by James Clear: A practical guide to building good habits and breaking bad ones, tailored for personal and professional growth.
   - "The Lean Startup" by Eric Ries: A must-read for entrepreneurs looking to build agile and successful ventures.
   - "Good to Great" by Jim Collins: Discover the strategies that turn good companies into industry leaders.
   - "Blue Ocean Strategy" by W. Chan Kim and Renée Mauborgne: Learn how to create uncontested market spaces and render competition irrelevant.

2. Influential Articles:
   - "Why Startups Fail" by Harvard Business Review: An analytical breakdown of common pitfalls and how to avoid them.
   - "The State of Entrepreneurship in 2025" by Forbes: A forward-looking piece that outlines emerging opportunities and challenges.

3. Inspirational Case Studies:
   - The Story of SpaceX: From near bankruptcy to redefining the space industry, Elon Musk's journey with SpaceX is a testament to the power of vision and perseverance.
   - Warby Parker's Disruption of Eyewear: This case study highlights how two entrepreneurs challenged the status quo by offering affordable, stylish eyewear directly to consumers.
   - The Rise of Canva: Founders Melanie Perkins and Cliff Obrecht transformed graphic design by creating an intuitive platform accessible to all, achieving a multibillion-dollar valuation.

4. Podcasts and Audiobooks:
   - "How I Built This" by Guy Raz: Features interviews with the founders of some of the world's best-known companies.
   - "The Tim Ferriss Show": Offers deep dives into the habits and tactics of top performers across various fields.

5. Documentaries:
   - "The Social Dilemma": Explores the unintended consequences of social media and its impact on businesses and individuals.
   - "Inside Bill's Brain: Decoding Bill Gates": A glimpse into the mind of one of the world's most successful entrepreneurs.

By engaging with these resources and reflecting on the lessons shared, you can unlock new perspectives, refine your strategies, and fuel your entrepreneurial journey with renewed vigor.

These appendices are designed to serve as a comprehensive resource for entrepreneurs navigating the challenges and opportunities of 2025. Whether you're seeking practical tools, insights into future trends, or a dose of inspiration, you'll find valuable guidance to propel your success.

www.ingramcontent.com/pod-product-compliance
Lightning Source LLC
Chambersburg PA
CBHW071109240526
45469CB00006BD/2406